The Social Business Blueprint

Marketing Savvy in the Digital Age

By Michael Baird

Table of Contents

The Importance of Social Media in Business

In an era dominated by technology and digital connectivity, the role of social media in business has grown from being a mere option to an absolute necessity. It has become a powerful tool that transcends geographical boundaries, connecting businesses with their target audiences and fostering unprecedented growth. This essay explores the profound importance of social media in the modern business landscape.

Social media platforms offer businesses a global stage to showcase their products or services. With billions of users on platforms like Facebook, Instagram, Twitter, and LinkedIn, companies can tap into a vast and diverse audience. This expanded reach allows even small businesses to compete on a global scale, leveling the playing field and democratizing the business landscape.

In the digital age, a strong brand identity is vital for success. Social media provides a platform for businesses to define and communicate their brand personality, values, and mission. Consistent branding across social channels helps establish trust, credibility, and recognition among consumers.

Social media enables real-time, two-way communication between businesses and their customers. Companies can respond to inquiries, address concerns, and receive feedback promptly. This direct engagement fosters a sense of community and builds customer loyalty.

One of the most significant advantages of social media is its ability to target specific demographics and interests. Advanced advertising tools allow businesses to create highly tailored campaigns, ensuring their content reaches the most relevant audience. This not only improves conversion rates but also optimizes advertising budgets.

Through content marketing, businesses can demonstrate their expertise in their respective fields. By sharing valuable information, insights, and industry trends, companies position themselves as thought leaders. This not only establishes credibility but also attracts an engaged and loyal audience.

Social media has transformed the business landscape, offering a myriad of opportunities for growth and success. Its role in expanding reach, building brand identity, engaging with customers, enabling targeted marketing, and showcasing expertise cannot be overstated. Embracing social media is not just a choice for businesses; it is an essential strategy for thriving in the digital age.

The Value of Meta (Facebook) Ads

Meta ads are an invaluable tool for building brand awareness due to their reach, targeting capabilities, and ability to engage with a broad and diverse audience. Here's an explanation of why Meta ads are essential for brand awareness:

1. **Vast User Base:** Meta is one of the largest social media platforms globally, with billions of active users. This extensive user base provides an enormous opportunity to introduce your brand to a wide and diverse audience.

2. **Precise Targeting:** Meta offers powerful targeting options that allow you to reach specific demographics, interests, behaviors, and locations. You can define your ideal audience, ensuring that your brand message reaches the right people who are more likely to be interested in your products or services.

3. **Cost-Effective Advertising:** Compared to traditional advertising channels, Meta ads are often more cost-effective. You can set your budget and bidding strategy to control costs and maximize your return on investment (ROI).

4. **Visual and Engaging Content:** Meta ads support various ad formats, including images, videos, carousels, and slideshows. Visual content tends to be more engaging and memorable, making it an excellent medium for brand storytelling.

5. **Storytelling Opportunities:** Meta allows you to tell your brand's story and convey your unique value proposition. You can share your company's history, mission, values, and

customer success stories, which can resonate with your target audience and create a lasting impression.

6. **Consistent Branding:** Through Meta ads, you can maintain a consistent brand image by using your logo, colors, and messaging consistently. This consistency helps in reinforcing brand recognition and trust among your audience.

7. **Engagement and Interaction:** Meta provides features like comments, likes, and shares that encourage user engagement. Positive interactions with your ads can amplify your brand message as they appear in users' newsfeeds and extend your reach organically.

8. **Retargeting:** Meta allows you to retarget users who have previously interacted with your brand or website. This is a powerful way to keep your brand top of mind for potential customers who may not have converted initially.

9. **Custom Audiences:** You can create custom audiences based on your existing customer data, such as email lists, website visitors, or app users. This enables you to re-engage with past customers and nurture brand loyalty.

10. **Insightful Analytics:** Meta provides detailed analytics and performance metrics, allowing you to track the effectiveness of your brand awareness campaigns. You can measure metrics like reach, impressions, engagement, and click-through rates to evaluate the impact of your ads.

11. **Mobile-Friendly:** Meta is predominantly accessed via mobile devices, making it an ideal platform to reach users on smartphones and tablets. Mobile optimization ensures your brand is visible to users across various devices and locations.

12. **Ad Flexibility:** You have the flexibility to adjust your ad campaigns in real-time. If you notice an ad isn't performing as expected, you can make changes to optimize it, ensuring your brand message is as effective as possible.

Meta ads play a pivotal role in building brand awareness by leveraging the platform's vast user base, precise targeting options, cost-effectiveness, and engaging ad formats. By utilizing Meta's tools and features, you can effectively reach and resonate with your target audience, creating a strong and memorable brand presence in the digital landscape.

How to Create a Meta (Facebook) Ad

Creating a Meta ad involves a series of structured steps to effectively promote your business or message to a wide audience. Meta's user-friendly Ad Manager platform is your gateway to this process, offering a range of tools and settings to fine-tune your ad campaign. Below is a comprehensive guide on how to create a Meta ad:

1. **Log into Meta Business Manager:** To embark on your ad creation journey, you must first possess a Meta Business Manager account. If you don't have one yet, it can be conveniently set up by visiting business.Meta.com and following the provided setup instructions.

2. **Access Ads Manager:** Once you've successfully logged into your Business Manager account, navigate to the "Ads Manager" option located in the left-hand menu. Clicking this will grant you access to the Ad Manager dashboard, your hub for managing your ads.

3. **Choose Your Marketing Objective:** Meta offers a variety of marketing objectives tailored to different campaign goals. Select the one that best aligns with your desired outcome. These objectives encompass options like:
    - Brand Awareness: Promoting your brand to a wider audience.
    - Traffic: Driving users to your website.
    - Engagement: Encouraging likes, comments, and shares.
    - Conversions: Inspiring users to take specific actions, like making a purchase.
    - Catalog Sales: Showcasing your product catalog to potential customers.

- Lead Generation: Collecting contact information for future marketing.
- App Installs: Encouraging users to download your app.
- Video Views: Maximizing the visibility of your video content, and more.

4. **Set Up Your Ad Campaign:** This is where you define the parameters of your advertising initiative:
- Campaign Name: Give your campaign a descriptive name for easy reference.
- Target Audience: Specify the demographics, interests, behaviors, and locations of the audience you want to reach.
- Budget and Schedule: Determine your budget and decide whether you want to set a daily budget or a lifetime budget. Also, configure the ad delivery schedule.

5. **Choose Ad Placement:** Decide where your ads should appear, whether on Meta, Instagram, Audience Network, Messenger, or all of them. You can also opt for automatic placements, letting Meta optimize ad placement for you based on performance.

6. **Create Your Ad:** Craft the visual and textual components of your ad:
- Ad Format: Select the format that suits your content, such as single image, video, carousel, slideshow, and more.
- Creative Content: Upload images, videos, and text that resonate with your target audience.
- Ad Copy and Headlines: Write compelling ad copy and headlines to capture attention.
- Call to Action (CTA): Choose a CTA button that encourages users to take the desired action (e.g., "Learn More," "Shop Now," "Sign Up").

- Preview: Review how your ad will appear on various devices.

7. Set Up Tracking and Conversion Events (if applicable): If you have a website or app, implement Meta Pixel or App Events to track specific user actions following ad clicks, such as purchases, sign-ups, or other conversions.

8. Review and Confirm: Before launching your campaign, double-check all the details, including targeting parameters, budget allocation, and ad content. Then, click "Submit" or "Confirm" to set your ad campaign in motion.

9. Monitor and Optimize: Once your campaign is live, diligently monitor its performance within Ads Manager. Use the data gathered to make informed decisions and fine-tune various aspects of your campaign, including targeting, ad creative, budget allocation, and more, to enhance results.

10. Scale or End Your Campaign: Depending on your campaign objectives and performance metrics, you can choose to increase your ad spend to scale the campaign or conclude it when it has achieved its intended goals.

Remember that Meta's advertising platform is continuously evolving, so staying updated with the latest features and adhering to Meta's advertising policies and guidelines are crucial for maintaining successful ad campaigns.

How To Track Your Metrics on Meta (Facebook)

Evaluating the effectiveness of your Meta ads and making informed decisions to enhance your ad campaigns is a critical part of digital advertising. Meta offers a range of tools and metrics to assist you in tracking and analyzing your ad performance. Here's a more detailed explanation of how to effectively track your Meta ads:

1. **Meta Ads Manager:**
   - To begin tracking your Meta ads, log in to your Meta Business Manager account, which serves as the control center for your advertising efforts.
   - Access the Ads Manager section, which is the hub where you can manage and analyze your ad campaigns.
   - Select the specific ad campaign you want to track within Ads Manager.

2. **Key Metrics to Monitor:**

   - Reach: This metric shows you the number of unique individuals who have seen your ad. It helps gauge the overall visibility of your ad campaign.
   - Clicks: Track the number of clicks your ad receives. It indicates the level of user engagement with your content.
   - Impressions: This represents the total count of times your ad has been displayed to users, providing insights into how frequently it's being viewed.
   - Click-Through Rate (CTR): CTR is a percentage that reveals the proportion of users who clicked on your ad after viewing it. It's calculated by dividing the number of clicks by the number of impressions and helps assess ad relevance.

- Conversion Rate: Measure the percentage of users who completed a desired action after clicking your ad, such as making a purchase or signing up for a newsletter.
- Cost per Click (CPC): This metric calculates the average cost incurred for each user click on your ad.
- Cost per Conversion: Determine the average cost associated with each conversion event, such as a purchase. It helps evaluate the efficiency of your ad spend.
- Return on Ad Spend (ROAS): ROAS compares the revenue generated from your ads to the amount you've spent. It's a crucial metric for assessing the profitability of your advertising efforts (ROAS = Revenue / Ad Spend).

3. Customize Columns:
- Meta's Ads Manager allows you to tailor the displayed metrics according to your specific campaign objectives. You can customize columns to focus on the most relevant data for your analysis. Simply click on the "Columns" dropdown and select the metrics that are pertinent to your campaign.

4. Time Frame:
- Adjust the time frame to view data for specific periods. You can analyze performance for today, yesterday, the past week, or set a custom date range. This feature helps you spot trends and changes over time.

5. Breakdowns:
- Utilize breakdowns to segment your data by various dimensions, such as age, gender, location, device type, and more. This segmentation allows you to identify which audience segments perform best, helping you refine your targeting.

6. A/B Testing:

- If you're running multiple ad variations, Meta provides the option to conduct A/B tests (split tests). This enables you to compare different creatives, headlines, or audience segments to determine which performs most effectively.

7. Conversion Tracking:
- For websites and apps, it's essential to set up Meta Pixel or App Events. These tools track specific user actions post-ad click, such as purchases or sign-ups. This data is invaluable for measuring your campaign's impact on your desired outcomes.

8. Budget and Schedule Monitoring:
- Keep a close watch on your ad spend to ensure it aligns with your allocated budget. Adjust your budget settings as needed to avoid overspending.

9. Optimization:
- Take advantage of Meta's optimization features. These tools automatically allocate your budget to the highest-performing ads and target audiences, aligning with your campaign objectives for maximum efficiency.

10. Experiment and Adjust:
- Use the data you gather to make informed adjustments to your ad campaigns. Consider refining your ad creative, targeting criteria, bidding strategy, and budget allocation based on performance trends.

11. Export Data:
- If you require more in-depth analysis, you can export your ad performance data for further examination using external tools like Excel or Google Sheets.

12. Reports:

- To stay informed without constant monitoring, create and schedule reports within Meta Ads Manager. This allows you to receive regular updates on your ad campaign's performance via email.

Tracking and analyzing your Meta ad performance is essential for optimizing your campaigns and achieving your advertising objectives. By making data-driven decisions and regularly reviewing your metrics, you can refine your targeting, creative elements, and overall strategy to improve the effectiveness of your Meta ads.

The Value of Instagram Ads

Instagram
Instagram ads are a valuable tool for building brand awareness due to their visual nature, engagement opportunities, and ability to reach a highly active and diverse user base. Here's an explanation of why Instagram ads are important for brand awareness:

1. **Visual Appeal:** Instagram is a highly visual platform where images and videos take center stage. This makes it ideal for showcasing your brand's products or services in an aesthetically pleasing and compelling manner. Visual content tends to be more engaging and memorable, making it an effective way to capture the attention of your audience.

2. **Large and Active User Base:** Instagram boasts over a billion active users worldwide. This vast user base provides an extensive reach, allowing your brand to connect with a wide and diverse audience, including potential customers who may not be aware of your brand yet.

3. **Precise Targeting:** Like Facebook, Instagram offers robust targeting options, allowing you to define your ideal audience based on demographics, interests, behaviors, and locations. This precise targeting ensures that your brand message reaches the most relevant users who are likely to be interested in your offerings.

4. **Storytelling Opportunities:** Instagram provides various formats for storytelling, including photo and video captions, Stories, and IGTV. These formats enable you to convey your

brand's story, values, and mission in a visually compelling way, fostering a deeper connection with your audience.

5. **Engagement and Interaction:** Instagram encourages user engagement through features such as likes, comments, shares, and direct messages. Positive interactions with your ads can extend your brand's reach organically as they appear in users' feeds and stories, amplifying your brand message.

6. **Instagram Shopping:** For e-commerce brands, Instagram offers a seamless shopping experience through features like Shopping Tags and the Shop tab. Users can easily discover and purchase products directly from your ads, streamlining the path to conversion.

7. **Influencer Partnerships:** Instagram is a hub for influencer marketing. Collaborating with relevant influencers in your industry or niche can help expose your brand to their followers, increasing brand awareness through trusted recommendations.

8. **Visual Consistency:** Consistency in visual branding is essential for brand recognition. Instagram allows you to maintain a cohesive brand image by using consistent colors, filters, and visual elements across your posts and ads.

9. **Analytics and Insights:** Instagram provides detailed analytics and insights about your ad campaigns. You can track metrics like reach, impressions, engagement, and website clicks to gauge the effectiveness of your brand awareness efforts and make data-driven decisions.

10. **Multiple Ad Formats:** Instagram offers various ad formats, including photo ads, video ads, carousel ads, and

story ads. This diversity allows you to experiment with different content types and find the most engaging format for your brand message.

11. **Cross-Platform Integration:** Instagram is owned by Facebook, and its ad platform is integrated with Facebook Ads Manager. This integration simplifies ad campaign management and allows you to leverage your Facebook targeting data on Instagram.

12. **Mobile-First Audience:** Instagram is primarily accessed on mobile devices, making it an excellent platform to reach users on smartphones and tablets. Mobile optimization ensures your brand is visible to users across various devices and locations.

Instagram ads are instrumental in building brand awareness by leveraging the platform's visual nature, large user base, precise targeting options, and engagement features. By effectively using Instagram's tools and features, you can create a visually appealing brand presence that resonates with your target audience and fosters recognition and trust in the digital landscape.

How to Create an Instagram Ad

Instagram ads are highly valuable for building brand awareness due to their visual nature, extensive reach, and engagement capabilities. Here are key reasons why Instagram ads are crucial for brand awareness:

1. **Visual Appeal:** Instagram is a visual platform, primarily focused on images and videos. This makes it an ideal platform for showcasing your brand's products, services, and aesthetic in a visually captivating way. Visual content tends to leave a lasting impression and is more likely to be shared and remembered.

2. **Large and Active User Base:** Instagram boasts over a billion monthly active users. This massive user base provides an extensive audience to introduce your brand to. Whether you're targeting a local or global audience, Instagram offers the potential to reach a diverse and engaged community.

3. **Precise Targeting:** Instagram's advertising platform, integrated with Facebook Ads Manager, offers precise targeting options. You can define your ideal audience based on demographics, interests, behaviors, and locations. This ensures that your brand message reaches users who are most likely to be interested in what you offer.

4. **Engagement Opportunities:** Instagram provides a variety of engagement features, including likes, comments, shares, and direct messages. Positive interactions with your ads can significantly amplify your brand message as they appear in users' feeds and stories, leading to increased exposure and awareness.

5. **Storytelling:** Instagram offers various formats for storytelling, such as photo captions, Stories, IGTV, and Carousel ads. This enables you to tell your brand's story, showcase your mission, values, and unique selling points, fostering a deeper connection with your audience.

6. **Influencer Collaboration:** Instagram is a hub for influencer marketing. Partnering with relevant influencers allows you to leverage their existing followers to introduce your brand. This can be highly effective in building trust and awareness among their engaged audience.

7. **Mobile-Friendly:** Instagram is primarily accessed through mobile devices, making it an excellent platform to reach users on smartphones and tablets. Mobile optimization ensures that your brand is visible to users across various devices and locations.

8. **Integrated Shopping:** Instagram offers shopping features like Shopping Tags and the Shop tab, making it convenient for users to discover and purchase products directly from your ads. This streamlined shopping experience can increase brand exposure and sales.

9. **Analytics and Insights:** Instagram provides detailed analytics and insights about your ad campaigns. You can track metrics like reach, impressions, engagement, and website clicks. These insights help you evaluate the effectiveness of your brand awareness efforts and make data-driven decisions.

10. **Customization and Creativity:** Instagram ads allow for creative customization. You can experiment with various ad

formats, visuals, captions, and CTAs to create compelling and unique brand experiences that resonate with your audience.

11. **Consistency:** Maintaining a consistent visual brand identity on Instagram helps reinforce brand recognition. Consistency in the use of colors, filters, and visual elements across posts and ads contributes to a strong and memorable brand presence.

Instagram ads are essential for building brand awareness by leveraging the platform's visual nature, vast user base, precise targeting, engagement features, and storytelling capabilities. By effectively using Instagram's advertising tools and features, you can create a visually appealing brand presence that resonates with your target audience and fosters recognition and trust in the digital landscape.

How To Track Your Metrics on Instagram

Tracking the performance of your Instagram ads is crucial to assess their effectiveness and make informed decisions to optimize your ad campaigns. You can track Instagram ads using Facebook Ads Manager, as Instagram is owned by Facebook. Here's a step-by-step guide on how to track Instagram ads:

Note: Before you begin, make sure you have created and launched your Instagram ad campaign through Facebook Ads Manager.

1. **Access Facebook Ads Manager:**

   - Log in to your Facebook Business Manager account.
   - Click on "Ads Manager" in the left-hand menu to access the Ads Manager dashboard.

2. **Select Your Ad Campaign:**

   - In Ads Manager, locate and select the specific ad campaign that includes your Instagram ads.

3. **View Ad Performance Metrics:**

   - Once you've selected your ad campaign, you'll be able to view a summary of the ad performance metrics for all the ad sets and ads within that campaign. These metrics include reach, impressions, engagement, click-through rate (CTR), and more.

4. Customize Columns:

- You can customize the columns in Ads Manager to display the specific metrics that matter most to your campaign. Click on the "Columns" dropdown and choose the metrics you want to track, such as conversions, ad spend, and more.

5. Time Frame:

- Adjust the time frame to view data for specific periods. You can analyze performance for today, yesterday, the past week, or set a custom date range. This helps you identify trends and changes in ad performance over time.

6. Breakdowns:

- Use the "Breakdown" feature to segment your data by various dimensions, such as age, gender, location, device type, and more. This segmentation allows you to identify which audience segments are performing best and which need optimization.

7. Conversion Tracking:

- If your campaign's goal is to drive specific actions on your website, such as purchases or sign-ups, ensure that you have set up conversion tracking. This involves adding the Facebook Pixel to your website and configuring it to track the desired conversion events.

8. Budget and Schedule Monitoring:

- Keep a close eye on your ad spend to ensure it aligns with your allocated budget. You can adjust your daily or lifetime budget as needed to control costs.

9. **Optimization:**

- Facebook Ads Manager offers optimization options that automatically allocate your budget to the best-performing ads and target audiences based on your campaign objectives. Regularly review and adjust your optimization settings to improve performance.

10. **Experiment and Adjust:**

- Based on the data you gather, make data-driven adjustments to your ad campaigns. This may include refining your ad creative, targeting criteria, bidding strategy, and budget allocation.

11. **Export Data:**

- If you need to perform more in-depth analysis, you can export your ad performance data from Facebook Ads Manager. Exported data can be further analyzed using external tools like Excel or Google Sheets.

12. **Reports:**

- Create and schedule reports within Facebook Ads Manager to receive regular updates on your ad campaign performance via email. Reports provide a convenient way to track performance without having to log in to the platform frequently.

By regularly monitoring and analyzing the performance of your Instagram ads in Facebook Ads Manager, you can make informed decisions to optimize your campaigns, improve targeting, creative elements, and overall strategy, ultimately achieving your advertising goals and building brand awareness effectively.

Creating an Instagram ad involves several steps and can be done through Facebook Ads Manager, as Instagram is owned by Facebook. Here's a step-by-step guide on how to create an Instagram ad:

Note: Before you begin, make sure you have a Facebook Page linked to your Instagram account and access to Facebook Ads Manager. You should also have clear objectives and creative assets ready for your ad.

1. **Access Facebook Ads Manager:**

- Log in to your Facebook Business Manager account. If you don't have one, you can create it by visiting business.facebook.com and following the setup instructions.
- Click on "Ads Manager" in the left-hand menu. This will take you to the Ads Manager dashboard.

2. **Select Your Campaign Objective:**

- In Ads Manager, click the "+ Create" button to start a new ad campaign.
- Choose your marketing objective. For brand awareness, you might select objectives like "Brand Awareness," "Reach," or "Traffic."

3. **Set Up Your Campaign:**

- Give your campaign a name for easy reference.
- Define your target audience by specifying demographics, interests, behaviors, and locations.
- Set your campaign budget and schedule. You can choose a daily budget or a lifetime budget, and you can specify the start and end dates for your campaign.

4. Choose Placements:

- Instagram ads can be placed on Instagram only, or you can select "Automatic Placements" to have Facebook optimize ad placement across various platforms. To specifically target Instagram, uncheck other options.

5. Create Your Ad Set:

- Name your ad set for organizational purposes.
- Define your budget allocation for this ad set.
- Set the schedule for when you want your ads to run.
- Configure the ad delivery optimization to align with your campaign goals (e.g., link clicks, impressions).

6. Create Your Ad:

- In the ad set, click on "+ Create" to design your Instagram ad.
- Select your Instagram account from the dropdown if it's not pre-selected.
- Choose the ad format you want to use, such as single image, single video, carousel, or story ad.
- Upload your creative assets, which typically include images or videos. Ensure they meet Instagram's ad specifications regarding resolution, aspect ratio, and file format.
- Add compelling ad copy and headlines to convey your brand message effectively.
- Configure your Call to Action (CTA) button, such as "Learn More," "Shop Now," or "Sign Up."
- Preview your ad to see how it will look on Instagram across different devices.

7. Set Up Tracking and Conversion Events (if applicable):

- Add the Facebook Pixel to your website to track conversions. Define the specific conversion events you want to track, such as purchases, sign-ups, or other actions.

8. Review and Confirm:

- Carefully review all the details, including targeting, budget, ad content, and scheduling.
- Click "Submit" or "Confirm" to launch your Instagram ad campaign.

9. Monitor and Optimize:

- Once your ad campaign is live, regularly monitor its performance in Ads Manager.
- Make data-driven adjustments based on the metrics you gather, such as reach, impressions, click-through rate (CTR), and conversions.

10. Scale or End Your Campaign:

- Depending on your campaign objectives and performance, you can choose to scale up your ad spend or end the campaign when it has achieved its goals.

Remember to comply with Facebook and Instagram's advertising policies and guidelines, and ensure that your ad content aligns with Instagram's visual and creative standards for the best results in building brand awareness on the platform.

Best Practices When Creating a Graphic for Your Ad

Creating an effective graphic for an ad involves several best practices to ensure it captures the audience's attention and conveys the intended message effectively. Here are some key guidelines to follow:

1. **Know Your Audience:** Understand your target audience's preferences, interests, and demographics to create a graphic that resonates with them. I'll go into this one more later.

2. **Clear Message:** Your graphic should convey a clear and concise message. Avoid clutter and ambiguity.

3. **Eye-Catching Visuals:** Use high-quality images, graphics, and colors that grab attention. Make sure your visuals are relevant to your message.

4. **Branding:** Incorporate your brand elements such as logos, fonts, and colors to maintain consistency and increase brand recognition.

5. **Simplicity:** Keep the design simple and uncluttered. Avoid using too many elements or text that might overwhelm the viewer.

6. **Hierarchy:** Use visual hierarchy to guide the viewer's eye through the graphic. Important information should be prominent, while less important details should be less prominent.

7. **Color Scheme:** Choose a color scheme that aligns with your brand and conveys the right emotions. Consider color psychology to evoke specific feelings in viewers.

8. **Typography:** Select fonts that are easy to read and align with your brand's personality. Use a maximum of two or three fonts to maintain consistency.

9. **Whitespace:** Incorporate whitespace strategically to improve readability and overall aesthetics.

10. **Balance and Proportion:** Ensure a balanced composition and proper proportion of elements within the graphic.

11. **Mobile Optimization:** Given the prevalence of mobile devices, design your ad to be responsive and visually appealing on various screen sizes.

12. **Call to Action (CTA):** Include a clear and compelling CTA that tells viewers what you want them to do next. Use action-oriented language.

13. **A/B Testing:** Create multiple versions of your graphic and conduct A/B tests to determine which one performs best with your audience.

14. **Compliance:** Ensure your ad adheres to all relevant advertising regulations, especially when it comes to industries like pharmaceuticals, finance, or alcohol.

15. **Testimonials or Social Proof:** If applicable, include customer reviews or endorsements to build trust.

16. **Storytelling:** Use visuals that tell a story or evoke emotions related to your product or service. People often connect with narratives.

17. **Consistency Across Platforms:** If you plan to use the graphic across different advertising platforms, ensure it complies with each platform's guidelines and specifications.

18. **Tracking and Analytics:** Implement tracking mechanisms to measure the ad's performance and gather data for future improvements.

19. **Feedback:** Seek feedback from peers or target audience groups before finalizing the design to gain valuable insights.

20. **Legal Considerations:** Be aware of copyright and licensing issues related to images, fonts, and other elements used in your ad.

Remember that the effectiveness of an ad graphic can vary depending on the context and goals of your campaign. Continuously analyze and refine your designs based on performance data to achieve the best results.

Finding Your Audience for Your Product or Service

In the vast landscape of business and marketing, finding your target audience is like discovering a hidden treasure. Your product or service may be extraordinary, but if it doesn't reach the right people, it won't achieve its full potential. In this chapter, we'll delve into the strategies and techniques to uncover your audience effectively.

1. Market Research: The Foundation

Before you can find your audience, you need to know where to look. This is where market research comes in. Conduct thorough market research to understand your industry, competitors, and potential customers. Here are some key steps:

- Identify Your Unique Selling Proposition (USP): What sets your product or service apart from the competition? Understanding your USP helps you define your niche.

- Customer Personas: Create detailed customer personas based on demographics, interests, pain points, and behavior. This helps you visualize your ideal audience.

- Competitive Analysis: Study your competitors to see who they are targeting. Analyze their strengths and weaknesses to find gaps you can fill.

- Surveys and Feedback: Gather feedback from existing customers to refine your understanding of your audience.

2. Segmentation: Divide and Conquer

Not all customers are the same. They have different needs, preferences, and behaviors. Segment your audience into smaller, more manageable groups. Common segmentation criteria include:

- Demographics: Age, gender, income, education, location, marital status, etc.

- Psychographics: Lifestyle, values, interests, hobbies, and personality traits.

- Behavior: Purchase history, brand loyalty, online behavior, and engagement with your content.

- Needs and Pain Points: Identify the specific problems your product or service can solve for different segments.

3. Utilize Data and Analytics

Data is a goldmine for understanding your audience. Use analytics tools to track user behavior on your website or app. This data can reveal insights about your audience's preferences and how they interact with your content. Pay attention to metrics like:

- Website Traffic: Analyze which pages are most popular and how long visitors stay.

- Conversion Rates: Understand where and why customers drop off in your sales funnel.

- Social Media Insights: Study engagement metrics, audience demographics, and content performance.

- Email Campaign Data: Track open rates, click-through rates, and conversion rates to understand your audience's response.

4. Test and Iterate

Your understanding of your audience is not static. As you launch marketing campaigns and interact with customers, gather feedback and adapt your strategies. A/B testing can be a valuable tool for refining your approach. Try different messaging, visuals, and targeting options to see what resonates best.

5. Social Media Listening

Social media platforms are a treasure trove of information about your audience. Use social listening tools to monitor conversations related to your industry, brand, or products. Pay attention to the language and sentiments used by your audience. Respond to their questions and comments to build a relationship.

6. Partnerships and Influencers

Collaborate with influencers or businesses that already have an established audience similar to yours. This can help you tap into an existing community of potential customers.

7. Feedback Loops

Create channels for direct feedback from your customers. Encourage reviews, conduct surveys, and listen to customer support inquiries. This not only helps you improve your product but also deepens your understanding of your audience.

8. Stay Updated

Market dynamics change, and audience preferences evolve. Stay informed about industry trends, emerging technologies, and shifts in consumer behavior. Adapt your strategies accordingly.

Finding your audience is an ongoing process that requires a blend of research, analysis, and adaptation. It's about understanding your customers on a deep level and tailoring your marketing efforts to speak directly to their needs and desires. By investing the time and effort into this process, you'll be well on your way to building a loyal customer base that values what you offer. Remember, your audience is out there, waiting to be discovered, so keep exploring and refining your approach.

The Dream: Making a Post Go Viral

Creating a viral social media post is the dream of many marketers and content creators. While there's no guaranteed formula for making a post go viral, several factors can increase the likelihood of your content spreading rapidly across social networks. Here are key elements that contribute to a social media post going viral:

1. **Compelling Content:** Your content must be engaging, entertaining, informative, or emotionally resonant. It should evoke a strong reaction, such as laughter, awe, anger, or empathy. High-quality and unique content tends to stand out.

Example: A pet supply company creates a heartwarming video of a rescue dog's journey to finding a forever home, highlighting their products along the way. Viewers are emotionally engaged and share the video due to its touching narrative.

2. **Timing:** Timing matters. Posting when your target audience is most active on the platform can increase the initial visibility of your post. Use analytics tools to determine the best times to post.

Example: A fashion brand posts its new collection just before a major fashion event or during a seasonal trend, capitalizing on the heightened interest and engagement in fashion-related content.

3. **Relevance:** Your content should align with current trends, events, or conversations within your niche. If it's timely and relevant, it's more likely to capture attention.

Example: A fitness influencer releases a series of home workout videos during the COVID-19 lockdown when many people are seeking ways to stay active at home. The content is timely and addresses a current need.

4. **Visual Appeal:** Visual content, such as images, videos, and infographics, tends to perform well on social media. Make sure your visuals are eye-catching and well-designed.

Example: An art supply store shares visually stunning time-lapse videos of artists creating intricate artworks using their products. The striking visuals catch the eye and prompt shares among art enthusiasts.

5. **Short and Shareable:** Keep your content concise and easy to share. A brief, clear message is more likely to be shared than a lengthy one.

Example: A tech company creates a concise, visually appealing infographic that explains a complex concept in a simple and shareable format. Users easily share the infographic to educate their followers.

6. **Emotional Appeal:** Content that triggers strong emotions, whether positive or negative, tends to get shared more. People like to share content that reflects their feelings.

Example: A charity organization posts a video showcasing the heartwarming moment of a child receiving a life-changing gift. The emotions evoked by the video lead to widespread sharing and support.

7. **Storytelling:** Crafting a compelling narrative can make your content more shareable. Stories have a natural way of capturing people's attention and imagination.

Example: A food blog shares the journey of a chef discovering unique recipes from different cultures, weaving storytelling elements into each post. Followers eagerly await each new chapter.

8. **Use of Humor:** Humor is a powerful tool for viral content. If you can make people laugh, they're more likely to share your post with others.

Example: A fast-food chain creates a humorous video ad featuring funny scenarios involving their products. The humor encourages viewers to share the video with friends for a laugh.

9. **Incentives:** Running contests, giveaways, or challenges that encourage user participation and sharing can boost virality. People love the opportunity to win something or be part of a community.

Example: A cosmetics brand launches a social media challenge where users share creative makeup looks using their products. Participants have a chance to win a prize, motivating them to share their entries.

10. **User-Generated Content:** Encourage your audience to create and share content related to your brand or product. This fosters a sense of community and amplifies your reach.

Example: A tourism agency encourages travelers to share their vacation photos and experiences using a specific hashtag. The agency then shares these user-generated posts, creating a sense of community.

11. **Hashtags and Trends:** Use relevant hashtags to increase the discoverability of your content. Monitor trending topics and incorporate them into your posts when appropriate.

Example: A tech company joins a trending hashtag related to a new product launch event. By including the hashtag, their content becomes discoverable to a wider audience interested in the event.

12. **Influencer Collaboration:** Partnering with influencers who have a large and engaged following can give your content a significant boost.

Example: A fashion brand partners with a popular fashion influencer to showcase their latest collection. The influencer's endorsement and reach introduce the brand to a broader audience.

13. **Engagement and Interaction:** Respond to comments and engage with your audience. The more people interact with your post, the more it will be shown to others.

Example: A cosmetics company responds promptly to comments on their social media posts, engaging in conversations with followers. This interaction builds a loyal community around the brand.

14. **Platform-Specific Strategies:** Different social media platforms have their own nuances. Tailor your content and strategies to fit the platform you're using.

Example: A travel agency utilizes Instagram to showcase visually appealing travel destinations through high-quality images and Instagram Stories. They use LinkedIn to share professional travel advice for business travelers.

15. **Network Effect:** Virality often relies on the network effect, where one share leads to more shares. The more people who see and share your content, the faster it can go viral.

Example: A viral tweet about a humorous meme leads to thousands of retweets, and the meme spreads across Twitter rapidly as users share it with their followers.

16. **Luck:** Finally, and often most importantly, luck plays a role in virality. Sometimes, a post simply resonates with the right people at the right time and takes off unexpectedly.

Example: Sometimes, a simple, unexpected post, like a candid moment captured at an event, resonates with a broad audience due to its relatability or humor, leading to unexpected virality.

Not every post needs to go viral to be successful. The goal is to create consistent, high-quality content that resonates with your target audience and builds a loyal following over time. Virality should be seen as a bonus, not the primary objective.

Unlocking Success With Social Media Marketing

In today's digital age, the steps to market and advertise on social media have become more than just a recommended strategy; they are a fundamental necessity for businesses of all sizes. Social media platforms have evolved into bustling hubs of activity, teeming with opportunities for companies to engage with their target audiences, build brand presence, and ultimately drive growth.

Social media platforms are home to billions of active users worldwide. By establishing a presence on these platforms and following a strategic marketing plan, businesses can instantly access a vast and diverse audience. Whether you are a local shop or a global corporation, the potential to reach new customers and markets is unprecedented. Social media facilitates direct, real-time engagement with customers. It offers a platform for businesses to have meaningful conversations, address inquiries, and receive feedback promptly. This engagement fosters a sense of community and builds trust and loyalty among customers.

Compared to traditional advertising methods, social media marketing is remarkably cost-effective. Creating and sharing content on social platforms often requires minimal financial investment, making it accessible to businesses with varying budgets. Additionally, the ability to target specific demographics ensures that marketing dollars are spent efficiently. In addition to the low cost to produce ads, social media platforms provide a wealth of data and analytics tools that allow businesses to gain profound insights into their audience's behavior and preferences. By analyzing these metrics, companies can refine their strategies, improve content, and make informed decisions that drive better results.

In today's competitive business landscape, staying ahead of the competition is crucial. Those who master social media marketing gain a significant competitive advantage. They can adapt quickly to changing trends and customer preferences, ensuring their business remains relevant and innovative.

The steps to market and advertise on social media are not merely a means to an end; they are the lifeblood of modern business growth. Through what you've learned in this book, businesses can harness the immense power of social media platforms to reach new audiences, engage with customers, build their brand, make data-driven decisions, and stay ahead in an ever-evolving market. The benefits are clear: social media marketing is the key to unlocking success in the digital age. So what are you waiting for?